THE SKILLS OF PROFESSIONAL EVALUATION

THE SKILLS OF PROFESSIONAL EVALUATION

PSYCHIATRIC REHABILITATION PRACTICE SERIES: book 3

Mikal R. Cohen, Ph.D.
Director of Training, Center for Rehabilitation Research
  and Training in Mental Health
Research Associate Professor
Department of Rehabilitation Counseling
Sargent College of Allied Health Professions
Boston University

William A. Anthony, Ph.D.
Director, Center for Rehabilitation Research and
  Training in Mental Health
Associate Professor
Department of Rehabilitation Counseling
Sargent College of Allied Health Professions
Boston University

Richard M. Pierce, Ph.D.
Director of Training Services
Carkhuff Institute of Human Technology
Amherst, Massachusetts

Leroy A. Spaniol, Ph.D.
Director of Research and Evaluation, Center for
  Rehabilitation Research and Training in Mental
  Health
Assistant Professor
Department of Rehabilitation Counseling
Sargent College of Allied Health Professions
Boston University

John R. Cannon, Ph.D.
Director of Evaluation
Carkhuff Institute of Human Technology
Amherst, Massachusetts

University Park Press
Baltimore

UNIVERSITY PARK PRESS
International Publishers in Science, Medicine, and Education
233 East Redwood Street
Baltimore, Maryland 21202

This book was developed by the Carkhuff Institute of Human Technology, 22 Amherst Road, Amherst, MA 01002, pursuant to Public Health Service Grant No. T21 MH 14502-20 with the National Institute of Mental Health; Alcohol, Drug Abuse, and Mental Health Administration, Department of Health, Education and Welfare.

THE PSYCHIATRIC REHABILITATION PRACTICE SERIES

Instructor's Guide
by *William A. Anthony, Ph.D.,*
Mikal R. Cohen, Ph.D., and Richard M. Pierce, Ph.D.

Book 1: **The Skills of Diagnostic Planning** / *William A. Anthony, Richard M. Pierce, Mikal R. Cohen, and John R. Cannon*
Book 2: **The Skills of Rehabilitation Programming** / *William A. Anthony, Richard M. Pierce, Mikal R. Cohen, and John R. Cannon*
Book 3: **The Skills of Professional Evaluation** / *Mikal R. Cohen, William A. Anthony, Richard M. Pierce, Leroy A. Spaniol, and John R. Cannon*
Book 4: **The Skills of Career Counseling** / *Richard M. Pierce, Mikal R. Cohen, William A. Anthony, Barry F. Cohen, and Theodore W. Friel*
Book 5: **The Skills of Career Placement** / *Richard M. Pierce, Mikal R. Cohen, William A. Anthony, Barry F. Cohen, and Theodore W. Friel*
Book 6: **The Skills of Community Service Coordination** / *Mikal R. Cohen, Raphael L. Vitalo, William A. Anthony, and Richard M. Pierce*

Library of Congress Cataloging in Publication Data
Main entry under title:

The skills of professional evaluation.
  (Psychiatric rehabilitation practice series; book 3)
  Bibliography: p.
  1. Mentally ill—Rehabilitation. 2. Performance—
Evaluation. I. Cohen, Mikal R. II. Series.
[RC439.5.S56]   362.2'0425   79-29690
ISBN 0-8391-1576-8

THE SKILLS OF PROFESSIONAL EVALUATION ▰

CONTENTS

ABOUT THE AUTHORS

Dr. Mikal R. Cohen is the Director of Rehabilitation and Mental Health Services at the Carkhuff Institute of Human Technology, a non-profit organization dedicated to increasing human effectiveness. Dr. Cohen has been a practitioner in several outpatient and inpatient mental health settings, and has served as an administrator, inservice trainer, program evaluator and consultant to numerous rehabilitation and mental health programs. She has developed teaching curricula and taught the skills of psychiatric rehabilitation to practitioners throughout the United States. Furthermore, Dr. Cohen has authored a number of books and articles in the fields of mental health and health care.

Dr. William A. Anthony is an Associate Professor and Director of Clinical Training in the Department of Rehabilitation Counseling, Sargent College of Allied Health Professions, Boston University. Dr. Anthony has been Project Director of a National Institute of Mental Health grant designed to develop and evaluate training materials for persons studying and practicing in the field of Psychiatric Rehabilitation. Dr. Anthony has been involved in the field of Psychiatric Rehabilitation in several different capacities. He has researched various aspects of psychiatric rehabilitation practice and has authored over three dozen articles about psychiatric rehabilitation which have appeared in professional journals.

Dr. Richard M. Pierce is Director of Training Services at the Carkhuff Institute of Human Technology, a non-profit organization dedicated to increasing human effectiveness. Dr. Pierce has extensive counseling experience and has consulted to dozens of local, state and federal human service programs. He has taught the skills and knowledge of psychiatric rehabilitation to practitioners from a variety of disciplines. Dr. Pierce is noted for his research on the training of counselors. Dr. Pierce has authored eight books and dozens of articles in professional journals.

Dr. LeRoy Spaniol is an assistant professor in the Department of Rehabilitation Counseling, at Boston University. He has taught, written and consulted extensively in the area of evaluation since 1974. His specialty is the supervision and training of counselors and allied health professionals in evaluation and clinical skills. He has presented and coordinated more than forty workshops over the past three years in these areas.

Dr. John R. Cannon is Director of Evaluation at the Carkhuff Institute of Human Technology. Dr. Cannon has extensive experience in both psychology and mental health and has consulted to dozens of local, state and federal human service programs. He has delivered training programs on the skills and knowledge of psychiatric rehabilitation to practitioners from a variety of disciplines. Dr. Cannon is particularly noted for his evaluation studies of human service programs. He has authored ten books and over two dozen articles published in professional journals.

CARKHUFF INSTITUTE of HUMAN TECHNOLOGY

The Carkhuff Institute of Human Technology is intended to serve as a non-profit international center for the creation, development and application of human technology. The Institute, the first of its kind anywhere in the world, takes its impetus from the comprehensive human resource development models of Dr. Robert R. Carkhuff. Using these models as functional prototypes, the Institute's people synthesize human experience and objective technology in the form of a wide range of specific programs and applications.

We live in a complex technological society. Only recently have we begun to recognize and struggle with two crucially important facts: improperly used, our technology creates as many problems as it solves; and this same technology has been delivered to us with no apparent control or "off" buttons. Our attempts to retreat to some pretechnological, purely humanistic state have been both foolish and ill-fated. If we are to develop our resources and actualize our real potential, we must learn to grow in ways which integrate our scientific and applied knowledge about the human condition with the enduring human values which alone can make our growth meaningful.

We cannot afford to waste more time in fragmentary and ill-conceived endeavors. The next several decades — and perhaps far less than that — will be a critical period in our collective history. Recognizing this, the Carkhuff Institute of Human Technology is dedicated to fostering the growth and development of personnel who can develop, plan, implement and evaluate human resource development programs while making direct contributions to the scientific and technological bases of these same programs. Thus the Institute's fundamental mission is to integrate full technical potency with fully human and humane goals — in other words, to deliver skills to people which let them become effective movers and creators rather than impotent victims.

CARKHUFF of INSTITUTE HUMAN TECHNOLOGY

22 AMHERST ROAD
AMHERST, MA 01002
(413) 256-0169

PSYCHIATRIC REHABILITATION PRACTICE SERIES

PREFACE

This text is one of a series of six books designed to facilitate the teaching of various psychiatric rehabilitation skills. It is written for professionals practicing in the field as well as for students studying in such professions as nursing, rehabilitation counseling, occupational therapy, psychology, psychiatry, and social work. Each of these disciplines has contributed and will continue to contribute practitioners, researchers, administrators, and teachers to the field of psychiatric rehabilitation.

This series of training manuals evolved from a lengthy analysis of the practitioner skills that seemed to facilitate the rehabilitation outcome of persons with psychiatric disabilities. Under the sponsorship of the National Institute of Mental Health, each of these training manuals was developed and then field-tested on a group of rehabilitation mental health professionals and students. Based on the feedback of the training participants after the use of these skills with psychiatrically disabled clients, each training manual was revised. Thus, the content of the books reflects not only the authors' perspectives, but also the ideas of the initial group of training participants.

The ultimate purpose of this six-volume series is to improve the rehabilitation services that are presently offered to the psychiatrically disabled person. This training text is written for those practitioners whose rehabilitation mission is either: (1) to assist in the reintegration of the psychiatrically disabled client into the community; or (2) to maintain the ability of the formerly disabled client to continue functioning in the community and, in so doing, to prevent a reoccurrence of psychiatric disability. In other words, depending upon a client's particular situation, psychiatric rehabilitation practitioners attempt either to reduce their clients' dependence on the mental health system or maintain whatever level of independence the clients have already been able to achieve.

This mission can be accomplished when the focus of the psychiatric rehabilitation practitioner's concern is increasing the *skills* and *abilities* of the psychiatrically disabled client. More specifically, the rehabilitation practitioner works to promote the client's ability to employ those skills necessary to live, learn, and/or work in the community. Success is achieved when the client is able to function in the community as independently as possible.

Historically, the primary focus in psychiatric rehabilitation has been on the development of alternative living, learning, and working environments. In such environments, psychiatrically disabled clients have been provided settings in which they can function at a reduced level of skilled performance that is still higher than the level of functioning typically demanded in an institutional setting. In addition, these rehabilitation settings have provided a more humane, active, and "normal" environment within which clients can function. The hope has been that, over a period of time, the more positive environment of these rehabilitation settings might help many clients to improve their ability to function more independently and, in many cases, to actually leave the rehabilitation setting.

Within the last decade, however, rehabilitation has come to involve much more than the development, administration, and coordination of specific settings. Psychiatric rehabilitation practitioners can now assume a direct rehabilitation role by *diagnosing critical skill deficits* in their clients and *prescribing rehabilitation programs* designed to overcome these skill deficits. The development of rehabilitation settings that emphasize the skills and abilities of the clients has helped lay the foundation for this approach to psychiatric rehabilitation.

Although the greatest boon to rehabilitation within the mental health system has been the development of new and unique environmental settings as alternatives to institutional living, the most significant failure of psychiatric rehabilitation has been its inability to train the psychiatric rehabilitation practitioner thoroughly in rehabilitation skills. Professionals from a wide range of disciplines (e.g., counseling, nursing, psychiatry, social work, and psychology) engage in the practice of psychiatric rehabilitation. For the most part, however, these various disciplines have only the expertise developed in their own professions to bring to the field of psychiatric rehabilitation. Their training has lacked a specific set of rehabilitation skills to complement the expertise of their own disciplines.

The present series of psychiatric rehabilitation training texts, of which this volume is a part, is designed to help overcome the lack of specialized training in psychiatric rehabilitation. These training books focus on the specific skills areas that are designed to equip the psychiatric rehabilitation practitioner with the expertise necessary to promote the abilities of the psychiatrically disabled client, either by increasing the client's skills and by modifying the environment so as to better accommodate the client's present level of skilled behavior.

The first two training books help the psychiatric rehabilitation practitioner to become more proficient in *diagnosing* and *teaching* the skills that the client needs to function more effectively in the community. The third book provides the practitioner with the skills necessary to *evaluate* the outcome of her or his rehabilitative efforts. Training books four and five focus specifically on practitioner skills that have been the traditional concern of the rehabilitation practitioner — *career counseling* and *career placement* skills. The sixth training book focuses on ways in which the rehabilitation practitioner can *use the resources of the community* to better accommodate the client's present abilities and programming needs.

Although each text is part of a series of training books, each has been designed so that it may be used independently of the other. The six books included in the series are:

1. **The Skills of Diagnostic Planning**
2. **The Skills of Rehabilitation Programming**
3. **The Skills of Professional Evaluation**
4. **The Skills of Career Counseling**
5. **The Skills of Career Placement**
6. **The Skills of Community Service Coordination**

The skills-learning *process* within the training books involves an explain-demonstrate-practice format. That is, the practitioner is first explained the skill, is then shown examples of the skill, and finally is provided with suggestions on how to practice or do the skill. The practice suggestions include first practicing in a simulated situation and then actually performing the skill with a psychiatrically disabled client.

The first chapter of each training book overviews the specific practitioner skills that comprise that text. The next several chapters of each text are the teaching chapters and present the explain-demonstrate-practice steps involved in learning each specific skill. The final chapter of each book suggests ways in which the practitioner can evaluate one's own or another person's performance of these skills. The reference section of the books contains the major references that are sources of further discussion of various aspects of the skills.

Each of the major teaching chapters has a vignette at the beginning and end of the chapter. This vignette or short story is designed to illustrate unsuccessful and successful applications of the specific skills that are the focus of that particular chapter. Its purpose is to give the reader an overview of the skills that are presented in each chapter. In addition, a summary of the skill behaviors that comprise each major skill is given at the end of each chapter section.

Each chapter contains practice suggestions for each skill that can facilitate the learners' practice of their newly developing skills. Often the learner is first asked to practice and demonstrate her or his skill learning by filling out some type of table or chart. These charts can serve as an observable demonstration of the learner's mastery of a particular skill. Most of these various charts are not needed in the day-to-day application of these skills with actual clients. However, during the skill-learning process, these charts or tables are useful in demonstrating the learner's present level of skill mastery, either to the learner her or himself or to the learner's supervisors and teachers.

The skill-learning *outcome* of each of these training volumes is an observable, measurable cluster of practitioner skills. These skills are not meant to replace the skills of the various disciplines currently involved in the practice of psychiatric rehabilitation; rather, these skills are seen as complementary to the professional's existing skills. The additional use of these rehabilitation skills can play an extremely important role in improving the efficacy of psychiatric rehabilitation.

The Psychiatric Rehabilitation Practice Series has developed out of the contributions of a number of different people. We are particularly indebted to a great many students and practicing professionals, who, by virtue of their willingness to learn these skills and provide knowledge as to their effectiveness, have allowed us the opportunity to develop, refine, and revise these texts.

We would also like to acknowledge the individual instructors who taught the first group of students from these texts, and gave willingly of their time and talents in the development of this series.

These initial instructors were Arthur Dell Orto, Marianne Farkas, Robert Lasky, Patrice Muchowske, Paul Power, Don Shrey and LeRoy Spaniol.

Particular appreciation is expressed to Marianne Farkas, who not only taught these skills, but who also assisted in the editing and evaluation of these training texts.

Boston, Massachusetts

W.A.A.
M.R.C.
R.M.P.

THE SKILLS OF PROFESSIONAL EVALUATION

Chapter 1 THE PROFESSIONAL EVALUATION MODEL

Stated most broadly, the goal of psychiatric rehabilitation is to restore to clients their capacity to function in the community. Philosophically, this means that rehabilitation is directed at increasing the *strengths* of the clients so that they can achieve their maximum potential for independent living and meaningful careers. Although many traditional treatment approaches seek to prepare clients to function independently, the emphasis in traditional psychiatric treatment has typically been on the reduction of client discomfort by changing underlying personality structures, increasing client insights, and alleviating symptomatology.

Although the total treatment process for disabled psychiatric clients includes aspects of both traditional psychiatric treatment and psychiatric therapy and rehabilitation, it is important that these activities be separated conceptually so that the rehabilitation process receives the emphasis necessary to develop its own unique contribution to client care.

This text represents one of a series of books whose purpose is to define and teach the unique skills of psychiatric rehabilitation. The particular skill with which this book is concerned is that of *professional evaluation.*

THE DEFINITION, PURPOSE, AND APPLICATIONS OF PROFESSIONAL EVALUATION

WHAT PROFESSIONAL EVALUATION IS

For the purposes of this book, professional evaluation refers to the process by which psychiatric rehabilitation practitioners systematically develop goals important to their rehabilitation job, monitor their performance, and use the results of the evaluation to develop new direction. More specifically, this process entails: (1) developing and establishing priorities for client and administrative goals; (2) operationalizing the highest-priority goals and their related intermediary goals; (3) monitoring performance on the goals; (4) organizing and using the monitoring results; and (5) recycling the evaluation process to generate new client and administrative goals.

WHY PROFESSIONAL EVALUATION IS IMPORTANT

The need for the evaluation of social service programs has been well documented (Chu and Trotter, 1974; Spaniol, 1977; Suchman, 1967; Walker, 1972). Economic, administrative, and ethical considerations represent the major reasons for program evaluation (Suchman, 1967). The rationale for individual practitioner evaluation incorporates these same reasons; *however, the professional evaluation model is unique in that the practitioner evaluates his or her own performance on both client and administrative goals.*

Systematic evaluation of psychiatric rehabilitation efforts is mandated by today's economic situation. The current financial crisis of rehabilitation agencies has implications for individual practitioners. Practitioners today face the problems of job insecurity and lack of job opportunities. They must compete successfully for a potentially decreasing number of available jobs. Systematic practitioner evaluation is one way practitioners can help assure their economic security. The ability to describe the effectiveness of their rehabilitation efforts in clear and convincing terms can help them to secure and maintain a rehabilitation position.

Administrative considerations constitute another major reason for systematic professional evaluation. Professional evaluation incorporates goals important from both administrative and client perspectives. It can provide results needed for agencywide administrative use (e.g., demonstration of program effectiveness, selection of preferred client populations). Additionally, systematic professional

2

evaluation allows practitioners to administer or manage their case-load responsibilities more effectively. The evaluation process directly informs practitioners about their areas of effectiveness and ineffectiveness and thus enables them to modify and improve their delivery of services. By the same token, systematic professional evaluation allows practitioners to exert control over both their rehabilitation delivery to clients (e.g., client progress) and administrative demands (e.g., size of case load). It can help practitioners to manage the pressures (e.g., to see more clients and to better help each one) that so often inhibit professional performance. The organized results that come from systematic professional evaluation can be used to set directions and manage the multiple demands for the practitioner's time and energy.

Another reason for professional evaluation is related to the issue of professional ethics. Most practitioners want to offer their clients the best possible services within their agencies' realistic limitations. To offer the best services, they need to base their delivery on more than good faith. Systematic professional evaluation will provide a realistic foundation for effective service delivery to rehabilitation clients. By tying evaluation to client goals, the practitioner ensures that the evaluation results are potentially meaningful and beneficial to clients.

Systematic professional evaluation can be the most effective method of bringing about changes based on evaluation results. As the evaluator, the practitioner can assure that the evaluation results can and will be used. In traditional program evaluation, the administrators of rehabilitation programs or their designees are often the program evaluators. Yet the results of their evaluation are intended to help practitioners to improve their performances. Often they fail to achieve this purpose because the evaluation feedback is not understandable or useful to the practitioners (Spaniol, 1977). Evaluation attempts frequently fail because practitioners feel threatened and therefore resist either participating in the evaluation or using the evaluation results. Systematic professional evaluation is most effective because it increases the likelihood of the practitioner being motivated to use the results. It helps to assure that the practitioner will want to participate and will be equipped to participate in the evaluation and will want to improve his or her performance based on the evaluation results.

Systematic professional evaluation is also effective because the practitioner is in a unique position to help design and complete the evaluation procedures. The practitioner understands the rehabilitation process and can help make the evaluation procedures relevant to this process. The practitioner also has access to every aspect of the rehabilitation process and can best assume responsibility for ensuring that evaluation procedures are accurately completed. In essence, the rehabilitation practitioner can help ensure that the evaluation is effectively accomplished.

The skills of professional evaluation provide rehabilitation practitioners with the expertise to effectively evaluate their performances. It assures that practitioners will have the skills to set client and administrative goals, to monitor their performance, and to organize and utilize the evaluation results.

In summary, systematic professional evaluation offers practitioners many benefits. In general, the primary effect of the evaluation will be that the practitioner will be able to do a better job. This improved performance can lead to greater satisfaction and pride. As previously mentioned, the ability to describe their improved performance may also aid practitioners in gaining economic security and in developing their careers. Most important, systematic professional evaluation provides practitioners with an opportunity to monitor and improve their delivery of services, without the need for outside assistance.

WHEN PROFESSIONAL EVALUATION CAN BE USED

The psychiatric rehabilitation process begins with a diagnostic interview. The outcome of the interview is a diagnostic plan identifying the strengths, weaknesses, and goals of the client with respect to his or her particular living, learning, and/or working environments *(Book 1: The Skills of Diagnostic Planning)*. The client's rehabilitation goals may involve: (1) moving to a new environment that is more compatible with client's present level of skill functioning or provides opportunities for the client to learn new skills; or (2) learning new skills that will help the client to remain in the present environment or become ready for a move to a new environment.

The psychiatric rehabilitation process culminates with the development and implementation of rehabilitation programs that help the client to learn new skills and use these skills in the appropriate living, learning, or working environment *(Book 2: The Skills of Rehabilitation Programming)*. The development and implementation of skill acquisition and application programs help clients to achieve their rehabilitation goals.

The practitioner can make use of systematic professional evaluation skills at any time, once the rehabilitation process has been implemented. The existence of a rehabilitation diagnosis, goals, and programs makes it possible to evaluate the rehabilitation process systematically. Professional evaluation skills can be used to evaluate client goals that result in "real life" client independence benefit. The practitioner can also use professional evaluation skills to assess the intermediary goals related to the rehabilitation process itself.

Practitioners can begin evaluating their performances at the inception of the rehabilitation process. For example, the practitioner may wish to evaluate his or her ability to encourage clients to come in for first appointments. Similarly, practitioners can evaluate their performances at any time during the diagnostic interviewing, assessment, or programming process. The point at which practitioners evaluate their performances depends on the priorities of their client and administrative goals as well as on the amount of time the practitioner has available to focus on the evaluation.

Practitioners skilled in professional evaluation evaluate their performance with any number of clients. Practitioners may evaluate their performance for a specific number of clients, for a certain percentage of their case load, or for a particular client problem population.

The size of the agency for which the practitioner works

will influence but not limit the use of professional evaluation skills. If a practitioner works alone or in a very small agency, he or she will need to assume all the evaluative roles described in this book. In a larger agency, resources will usually be available to help the practitioner carry out the evaluation.

The amount of freedom that practitioners have in determining when to evaluate their own performance will no doubt be a function of the ongoing evaluation program of their agencies. If there is no ongoing evaluative effort within the agency, the practitioner will be free to decide how to evaluate his or her performance. If agencywide evaluation activities already exist, the practitioner will be limited to activities that conform to existing evaluation goals and procedures. The existence of an ongoing agencywide evaluation program can help as well as limit the practitioner. The agencywide program evaluation may be helpful in developing and establishing priorities for the goals, in designing and implementing the monitoring plan, and in developing a plan to use the results. It will be easiest, of course, for the practitioner to use systematic professional evaluation skills when such skills are supported by the rehabilitation agency.

A rehabilitation agency may possibly wish to adopt the professional evaluation model as its agencywide evaluation program. In such a case, the various tasks of systematic professional evaluation may be shared by the practitioners, the supervisors, and the administrators of the agency. Although originally designed to be completed individually by the practitioner, many of the evaluation steps can be done with others. For example, a group of practitioners may wish to work together to explore the goals important to their delivery of rehabilitation services. A group of practitioners and supervisors may wish to operationalize the goals. An agencywide staff meeting of practitioners, supervisors, and administrators might wish to explore and develop a plan to use the evaluation results.

In summary, systematic professional evaluation skills can be used at any time in the rehabilitation process. They can be used during or after the rehabilitation process, to evaluate client skill development or successful use of community environments. The practitioner can use these evaluative skills in a variety of ways, depending on the scope or development of agencywide evaluation efforts. Professional evaluation skills can be used by a single practitioner or jointly with other practitioners, supervisors, and administrators. The determining criterion is simply the point where goals need to be set and assigned priorities or the point where existing goals need to be evaluated so that the results can be used to improve practitioner performance.

THE STAGES AND SKILLS OF PROFESSIONAL EVALUATION

The book will discuss in detail how professional evaluation is accomplished. The present section will simply overview the stages involved. As stated previously, the ultimate goal of professional evaluation is for the practitioner to use the evaluation results to improve his or her performance on client and administrative goals.

To achieve this goal, the practitioner proceeds through three basic developmental stages. Table 1 presents an outline of the stages and skills of professional evaluation. In the inital stage, the practitioner develops a list of *client and administrative goals*. Client goals flow from the practitioner's understanding of the rehabilitation process; administrative goals are based on the agency's objectives and may require that the practitioner read various written materials and talk to administrators. The practitioner sets goals that are relevant to clients and that will meet administrative demands, needs, and wants.

There are essentially five types of client goals: *involvement; understanding; skill acquisition; skill utilization;* and *benefit*. From these five major areas, the practitioner generates a list of goals relevant to rehabilitation clients. Administrative goals can relate to the responsibilities of the practitioner, benefits for the clients, and the survival and growth of the rehabilitation agency. In setting administrative goals, the practitioner will explore the agency's mission, goals, values, and expectations.

Most practitioners will be able to identify numerous cli-

7

ent and administrative goals. Before practitioners can assess their performance, the goals need to be assigned priorities. The practitioner can establish priorities for the goals based on a number of criteria (e.g., urgency to the client or the agency, benefit to the client or the agency, consistency with the practitioner's job description, whether the goal is an outcome or a process goal). Once priorities have been established, the practitioner needs to select the highest-priority goals for evaluation. The number of goals selected will depend on the practitioner's evaluation skills and the amount of time available for evaluation efforts. At this point, the practitioner is ready to begin the second stage of professional evaluation.

Table 1. Stages and Skills of Professional Evaluation

I. SETTING REHABILITATION GOALS

    A. Developing a list of client and administrative goals

    B. Establishing priorities for the goals

II. MONITORING PERFORMANCE

    A. Identifying related intermediary goals

    B. Operationalizing the priority goals and related intermediary goals

    C. Developing and implementing a monitoring plan

III. DEVELOPING NEW DIRECTION

    A. Developing a scale to organize the results

    B. Developing and implementing a plan to use the results

    C. Recycling the evaluation process

During stage 2, the practitioner monitors his or her performance on the priority goals. In this stage, the practitioner identifies the intermediary goals related to the highest-priority goals, operationalizes the priority goals and the related intermediary goals, and then designs and implements a monitoring plan.

In other words, before evaluating his or her performance on the goals, the practitioner needs to determine the intermediary steps related to the achievement of the priority goals. For example, if the goal of "preventing client hospitalizations" is given highest priority, a related intermediary goal might be "acquiring community resource utilization skills." After all the intermediary goals related to the priority goals have been determined, both the priority goals and their related intermediary goals can be operationalized.

In the operationalizing process, the practitioner makes the priority and the intermediary goals both observable and measurable. The operationalized goal thus becomes capable of being monitored. The key to operationalizing goals is to specify the observable behavioral components of the goal and determine how the behaviors can be measured. For example, the goal of "preventing client hospitalizations" might be operationalized to "the percentage of clients who are still living outside a hospital one year after termination of the rehabilitation process."

The final step in monitoring practitioner performance on the goals is to develop and implement a monitoring plan. The monitoring plan specifies the monitor, the person whose behavior is to be monitored, the monitoring device, and the time and place for the monitoring. Once the monitoring plan has been implemented and the data collected, the third stage begins.

In stage 3 of the rehabilitation evaluation process, the practitioner first organizes the evaluation results. Initially, the practitioner develops a scale that designates five levels of achievement of the goal. The practitioner uses the scale to evaluate his or her performance in relation to a previously identified standard. Second, to use this new understanding of professional performance, the practitioner needs to develop and implement a plan or program to promote such usage. The plan to use the results depends on the practitioner's reasons for doing the evaluation. The main reason for using evaluation results is to improve delivery to clients. However, the results of the evaluation may sometimes be used by the practitioner to meet an administrative demand or to develop his or her own career. The reason or combination of reasons for doing the evaluation dictates the specific programs developed to make use of the evaluation results (e.g., to receive in-service training or to redefine administrative expectations).

Implementing a plan to use evaluation results requires the practitioner to use the rehabilitation program development and implementation skills described in detail in the second book of this series, *The Skills of Rehabilitation Programming*. The desired outcome of using the evaluation results becomes the goal of the program. The practitioner needs to develop the steps of the program and implement those steps to achieve the desired outcome.

To achieve the desired outcome, the practitioner first focuses on the continued evaluation of the same goals. The evaluation process is not recycled to other goals, and new goals are not set, until the practitioner is satisfied with performance on the previously evaluated goals. Then the practitioner can recycle the evaluation process to additional high-priority goals.

In summary, the practitioner determines the most important client and administrative goals, develops and implements the evaluation of his or her performance on the operationalized goals and related intermediary goals, and then uses the evaluation results to improve performance. Skilled effort in this area will minimize ineffective practitioner performance and maximize the benefits to the practitioner, the clients, and the rehabilitation agency. The remainder of this book will focus on professional evaluation skills for the rehabilitation practitioner.

This book is organized so that a number of examples of client and administrative goals are set and assigned priorities in Chapter 2. In Chapter 3, the related intermediary goals for the highest-priority goals are set, and the priority goals and related intermediary goals are then operationalized. The practitioner's performance is evaluated on a few of these goals, and the results is organized and used in Chapter 4. The entire professional evaluation process can then be recycled so that the practitioner's performance on some of the remaining high-priority goals can be evaluated. Professional evaluation is truly an ongoing process.

Chapter 2 SETTING REHABILITATION GOALS

SETTING REHABILITATION GOALS: AN UNSKILLED APPROACH

Ed was proud of the skills he possessed and was able to use in his work as a psychiatric rehabilitation practitioner. And his pride was, up to a point, entirely justified.

Ed knew how to get his clients involved in the process of their own rehabilitation. He realized, for example, that real client involvement required him to do more than just schedule appointments and assume that people would show up. Ed also knew how to interact responsively with his clients. He understood the difference between a practitioner who tries to impose his own judgment upon clients and a practitioner who responds to clients in terms of their own unique perspective and experiences.

When beginning his evaluation efforts, Ed decided that continued client involvement in the rehabilitation process was his most important goal. But this decision was to prove a little misleading.

The agency with which Ed worked was primarily concerned with the placement of rehabilitation clients in a variety of settings. Some were helped to become involved in specialized training programs. Some were placed directly in competitive employment situations. Some went into a local sheltered workshop. Ideally, each client was provided with placement assistance tailored to meet the needs of his or her particular rehabilitative situation.

In his present case load, Ed sensed there were many clients for whom placement would be a critical factor in determining their sustained involvement with the agency in general and himself in particular.

"My clients are in pretty good shape right now," he told himself, "but the whole thing could fall apart if they wound up somewhere that put too much pressure on them. The best place for them is a sheltered workshop."

So, during his sessions with clients, Ed played down the possibility of competitive employment and spoke per-

suasively of the merits of a sheltered setting. He listened to his clients' fears, and he encouraged them toward a cautious approach. In the end, the clients decided not to take too large a step. They decided the sheltered workshop idea would be "best" for them.

Ed was pleased. He felt that his clients would certainly be able to work well in a sheltered situation. And success there, he told himself, would ensure their willingness to continue sessions at the agency until such time as some final placement could be arranged.

Ed's handling of these cases was typical of the way in which he handled every case. He didn't realize the flaw in his approach until a conference one day with his supervisor.

"Ed, I'd like you to tell me a little about the goals you have in mind when you work with your clients," the supervisor said. So Ed gathered his thoughts together and tried to explain what he was doing and why.

"I see ..." The supervisor looked thoughtful. "You see your primary purpose as maintaining client involvement in the rehabilitative process."

Ed nodded vigorously. "Uh-huh. I mean, I've seen too many practitioners who see a client once, turn him or her off, and never get anywhere. For me, continued client involvement is a must if we're really going to help!"

Now the supervisor nodded. But she still looked thoughtful. "I see your point, of course. Client involvement is critical. Although you need to involve clients, in and of itself involvement really doesn't do much for clients. Simply meeting with a practitioner on a regular basis is not enough. What really counts is the tangible **progress** that the client makes. It seems many of your placements don't really challenge the clients. The clients may initially be relieved, but eventually their lack of progress becomes apparent. Let's work together to explore how you can both continue to involve clients and make more challenging placements."

The skills of professional evaluation are used by practitioners to develop and establish priorities for a list of goals;

to operationalize these goal and monitor their performance in achieving these goals; and to use the evaluation results to improve their rehabilitation performance. The first phase of professional evaluation involves completion of two steps: (1) developing a list of goals; and (2) establishing priorities for these goals.

DEVELOPING A LIST OF GOALS

To reiterate, the practitioner's initial evaluative task is to develop a list of goals. One way to generate such a list is to consider goals as they relate to rehabilitation clients and as they relate to the rehabilitation agency. *Clients goals* are concerned with what clients need, want, or achieve during the rehabilitation process. *Administrative goals* are related to supervisory or administrative requirements and demands that affect the practitioner. These two categories are not meant to be discrete or mutually exclusive. Although administrative concerns invariably revolve around such issues as budgeting, funding, or practitioner supervision, goals that are relevant to clients are also relevant to administrators (e.g., preventing client hospitalizations). Indeed, the shared concern among practitioners, administrators, and consumers for improving the quality of service to rehabilitation clients would seem to create a condition of shared, not conflicting, goals. The categorization of goals as client or administrative is a device to help the practitioner generate a list of goals.

DEVELOPING CLIENT GOALS

The development of client goals is based on the rehabilitation process described in this series of books. The use of the skills described in detail in the first and second books of the series, *The Skills of Diagnostic Planning* and *The Skills of Rehabilitation Programming,* will provide the practitioner with goals for an individual client.

Flowing from the rehabilitation process described in this series of books, the practitioner's major client goals are: (1) to *involve* clients in the rehabilitation process; (2) to help clients *understand* their strengths and deficits and to get them to agree to work on their deficits; (3) to help clients *learn* the skills necessary to function well in their living, learning, or working environment; (4) to help clients *use* the skills in the specific environment where they are needed; and (5) to help clients achieve the desired or needed *benefits* from utilization of the skills in the specific environment where they are needed.

These major client goals provide a classification system for generating client goals. The five types of client goals are broadly defined as follows:

1. *Client involvement goals:* having the client regularly meet with and actively participate with the practitioner in discussing relevant concerns

2. *Client understanding goals:* helping the client to understand, define, and operationalize his or her skill strengths, deficits, and goals; and having the client agree to work on a comprehensive list of skill goals

3. *Client skill-acquisition goals:* helping the client to learn the skills he or she needs and to demonstrate these skills at the goal level defined during the diagnostic planning process

4. *Client skill-utilization goals:* helping the client to use his or her skills at the defined goal level in the specific environment where they are needed

5. *Client benefit goals:* helping the client to achieve the long-term benefits that result from using his or her skills in living, learning, or working environments (often the goals that initially motivated the client to engage in the rehabilitation process).

Using this classification system, the practitioner can develop a list of client goals. As an example, Table 2 presents a client goals chart outlining the involvement, understanding, skill-acquisition, skill-utilization, and benefit goals for a practitioner working for a private acute or short-term psychiatric hospital rehabilitation program.

Table 2. Client Goals Chart

Involvement	Understanding	Skill Acquisition	Skill Utilization	Benefit
1. Clients show up for scheduled appointments.	1. Clients work to identify skill strengths and deficits.	1. Clients can demonstrate job acquisition skills (e.g., job interviewing).	1. Clients can achieve job placement.	1. Clients get positive on-the-job evaluation report from supervisors.
2. Clients explore problems at personal meaning level.	2. Clients help to operationally define skill strengths and deficits.	2. Clients can demonstrate independent living skills (e.g., budgeting).	2. Clients can move to independent living setting.	2. Clients keep job for at least one year.
3. Clients contact practitioner when there is a crisis.	3. Clients agree to work to reach the skill growth goals defined on their Client Assessment Charts.			3. Clients live independently for at least one year.
	4. Clients help to identify the steps that will lead to achievement of their skill growth goals.			

Practice Situations

As an example, develop some client goals for Conrad. Conrad is a practitioner who is working with chronic psychiatric clients who have been recently discharged from the state psychiatric hospital. These clients are part of a de-institutionalization program that is moving clients to community residences with the goal of supporting their living outside of the hospital. Use a format similar to the client goals chart pictured in Table 3 to practice setting client goals. Generate client involvement, understanding, skill-acquisition, skill-utilization, and benefit goals for Conrad. Before beginning, review the definitions of the five types of client goals and sample goals in Table 2. As an additional practice exercise, for your own rehabilitation job or a job with which you are familiar (state rehabilitation agency) complete a client goals chart similar to the one provided in Table 3. In doing so, you will be generating a list of potential client goals.

Table 3. Sample Format for Client Goals Chart

Involvement	Understanding	Skill Acquisition	Skill Utilization	Benefit

DEVELOPING ADMINISTRATIVE GOALS

Realistically, both job security and the potential for advancement require the practitioner to have goals that relate to meeting administrative concerns. Administrative goals, then, can be defined as the practitioner's goals for meeting the demands, needs, or wants of the supervisor or administrator of the agency.

Administrative goals may relate to the practitioner's job description, the rehabilitation of clients, or the survival and growth of the rehabilitation agency. Ideally, the goals related to the survival or growth of the agency merge with the goals related to the rehabilitation of clients. Recently, the demands of funding sources (e.g., National Institute of Mental Health, Rehabilitation Services Administration) have focused more on demonstrations of client rehabilitation as a prerequisite for continued or increased funding. Table 4 lists some sample administrative goals.

Table 4. Administrative Goals

1. Client job placements
2. Practitioner punctuality in keeping appointments with clients
3. Reduced client hospital recidivism
4. Increased amount of fees collected
5. Client involvement in rehabilitation process
6. Increased written client goals in files.
7. Increased client ability to live, learn, and work in the community
8. Increased client contact hours.
9. Client completions of academic or vocational training
10. Increased number of chronically disabled clients served

The demands, needs, or wants of agency administrators are reflected in the agency's mission, goals, values, and expectations. The complexity of developing administrative goals is determined by how clearly the agency's administration has defined and presented its mission, goals, values, and expectations to the practitioner. The agency may have clearly written statements of: (1) the *mission,* or overall purpose of the agency; (2) the *goals,* or desired annual agency achievement; (3) the *values,* or those things considered important by the agency; and (4) the *expectations,* or specific demands, needs, or minimally acceptable agency outcomes. Ideally, the agency will have provided the practitioner with an initial orientation to and ongoing education about the mission, goals, values, and expectations of the rehabilitation program. When the agency has clearly defined its goals, the practitioner can proceed to develop administrative goals.

In some agencies, however, the mission, goals, values, and expectations are implicitly rather than explicitly stated. This is often the case when the rehabilitation practitioner functions as a component in other than a psychiatric rehabilitation program (e.g., hospital program, mental health program). The practitioner may not have a clear understanding of the administration's goals for the rehabilitation process and its expectations of the practitioner. When the administration's definition of the mission, goals, values, and expectations are unclear, the practitioner needs skills to explore and understand the administration's demands, needs, or wants so that he or she can develop appropriate administrative goals.

The specific steps in this exploration process are: (1) to generate a list of questions to explore the agency's mission, goals, values, and expectations; (2) to obtain the answers through reading relevant materials and talking with administrators; and (3) to develop a list of administrative goals. Although the practitioner will want to understand and work to achieve the agency's mission, goals, values, and expectations, he or she will be most concerned with how these directly affect the agency's evaluation of his or her performance.

The practitioner can generate questions that will: (1)

define the agency's *mission,* or its conception of the overall purpose of the practitioner's job; (2) define the agency's *goal,* or those things the administrator wants the practitioner to accomplish during the year; (3) clarify the agency's *values,* or those things the administration considers important to practitioner functioning; and (4) clarify the agency's *expectations,* or the minimally acceptable outcomes the administration expects from the practitioner. Sample practitioner questions and their answers are presented in Table 5.

Two ways to obtain answers to these questions are to read relevant materials and to talk with administrators. Relevant materials may include statements of mission and goals, orientation materials, annual reports, in-service training manuals, needs assessments, evaluation reports, funding proposals, newsletters, newspaper articles, job descrptions, memos, or record-keeping forms. These documents can be read for explicit or implicit statements about the agency's mission, goals, values, and expectations. Of course, this process may also generate additional questions.

In talking with the agency's administrator and supervisors, practitioners may be more precise in their questioning. For example, the practitioner may ask: "What services are mandated by the funding source?" "What needs to be delivered to clients in order to keep or increase funding?"

It is important to remember that these questions are tools to help the practitioner to discover the administration's demands, needs, or wants and to set his or her administrative goals. Essentially, the classification of the administration's demands, needs, or wants as mission, goals, values, or expectations is important only to the extent that it helps the practitioner to set administrative goals. These terms may be used differently among practitioners. For example, "increased practitioner work level" may be classified as an expectation by one practitioner and as a value by another. The crucial point is that these terms are helpful in generating questions and organizing the answers the practitioner needs to set his or her administrative goals.

Combining the lists of client and administrative goals

Table 5. Questions and Answers for Developing Administrative Goals

	Questions	Answers
Agency Mission	1. Why does this agency hire psychiatric rehabilitation practitioners? 2. What is the overall purpose of the agency?	1. (a) mandated by federal government. (b) to prevent hospitalization of clients. 2. (a) to help clients live independently in community.
Agency Goals	1. What does the agency want the practitioner to accomplish this year?	1. (a) see more clients by use of group sessions. (b) reduce average time of seeing client to a maximum of 6-9 months' posthospitalization (c) increase personal contacts with potential employers.
Agency Values	1. What are the value considerations when deciding whether to hire an applicant for the job of practitioner? 2. What are the values underlying the agency?	1. (a) a prior work experience. (b) ability to relate to clients (c) previous work record. 2. (a) psychiatrically disabled clients can live independently in the community. (b) the community should work to achieve independent living goals for disabled clients

Questions	Answers
Agency Expectations	
1. How will the practitioner's performance be measured?	1. (a) number of client interviews.
	(b) client achievement of rehabilitation benefits (e.g., job placement).
	(c) client satisfaction.
2. What are acceptable practitioner results with his/her clients?	2. (a) clients don't cancel or fail to show for appointments.
	(b) clients stay out of the hospital.
	(c) clients get placed in job.
3. What are the expectations of the community or funding boards for the practitioner?	3. (a) cost efficiency and effectiveness.
	(b) availabilty of service.
	(c) relationship with many community resources.
	(d) positive community opinions.
	(e) reduced negative disturbances from clients.

will give the practitioner a comprehensive list of goals. However, before evaluating his or her performance in achieving these goals, the practitioner needs to establish priorities for them.

Practice Situations

Practice answering the questions provided in Table 6 for your agency or an agency with which you are familiar. Remember to talk with administrator or read materials as needed to obtain the answers to your questions.

Table 6. Practice Questions

	Questions	Answers
Agency Mission	1. Why does this agency hire psychiatric rehabilitation practitioners? 2. What is the overall purpose of the agency?	1. 2.
Agency Goals	1. What does the agency want the practitioner to accomplish this year?	1.
Agency Values	1. What are the value considerations when deciding whether to hire an applicant for the job of practitioner? 2. What are the values underlying the agency?	1. 2.
Agency Expectations	1. How will the practitioner's performance be measured? 2. What are acceptable practitioner results with his or her clients? 3. What are the expectations of the community or funding board for the practitioner?	1. 2. 3.

Table 7 lists sample administrative goals that were clarified by the answers to the questions in Table 5. Using a format similar to Table 7, list all the goals included in your answers to the questions from Table 6.

Table 7. Administrative Goals Developed from Questions and Answers

1. Helping clients to live independently in the community
2. Providing federally mandated services
3. Preventing client hospitalizations
4. Increased number of client interviews
5. Use of group sessions
6. Reduced length of rehabilitation to maximum of 6–9 months posthospitalization
7. Practitioner ability to relate to clients
8. Increased number of clients served
9. Clients achievement of rehabilitation benefits
10. Clients satisfaction
11. Reduced client "no-shows" and cancelations
12. Client job placements
13. Cost efficiency
14. Cost effectiveness
15. Availability of services
16. Relationships with many community resources and potential employers
17. Positive community opinion
18. Reduced negative disturbances from clients

DEVELOPING A LIST OF GOALS: A SUMMARY

Goal: To develop a list of goals appropriate to the rehabilitation process, with which the practitioner can evaluate his or her performance

1. Develop goals related to clients.

   Use the categories of client involvement, understanding, skill acquisition, skill utilization, and benefit to develop goals.

2. Develop goals related to the rehabilitation agency.

   Generate a list of questions to explore the agency's mission, goals, values, and expectations. Obtain the answers to the questions by reading relevant materials and talking with administrators. From the answers, develop a list of administrative goals.

ESTABLISHING PRIORITIES FOR THE GOALS

Having developed a list of goals, the practitioner has a picture of the areas important in evaluating his or her performance. However, as the sample client and administrative goals charts indicate, there are numerous goals. The busy practitioner obviously cannot evaluate and improve his or her performance on all the goals. Also, without determining the comparative importance of each goal, the practitioner will have no way to eventually compare his or her performance with the performance of other practitioners. For example, imagine that Practitioner A has a higher percentage of clients achieving rehabilitation goals than Practitioner B. Practitioner B, however, has a higher client satisfaction level. Without some method of establishing priorities for the goals, comparison of the performances of Practitioner A and Practitioner B is arbitrary.

The solution to the problem lies in establishing priorities for the client and administrative goals that have been developed. Priorities will also give the practitioner a clearer perspective on the conflicting pressures to both "do a good job" with clients and "see more clients."

The process of establishing priorities involves analyzing the goals from several perspectives: (1) urgency; (2) benefit, (3) the practitioner's job description; and (4) whether the goal is an outcome or a process goal.

In establishing priorities on the basis of urgency or need, the practitioner will want to ascertain if the client or agency will suffer negative consequences if the goal is not achieved. For example, urgency from the client's perspective might mean that the client will lose his or her job. Urgency from the agency's perspective might mean that the agency will lose a source of funding.

The second criterion for establishing priorities is the question of benefit to the client or the rehabilitation agency. The practitioner can evaluate the goals to determine which would significantly benefit the client or the agency. For example, from the client's perspective, a benefit may mean moving to a more desirable, independent living setting. From the agency's perspective, a benefit may mean achieving the projected annual goals.

The third criterion is the practitioner's job description. A job description reflects the agreement of services to be provided for the salary to be collected. The practitioner can consider the job description to determine what is legitimately required of him or her. Ethically, the practitioner will be concerned with those goals included in the description of his or her job responsibilities.

The fourth criterion involves the distinction between process goals and outcome goals. Goals may be classified as either process or outcome depending on whether they are end goals or intermediary goals that lead to the end goals. Theoretically, every goal can be considered either a process goal or an outcome goal depending on the rehabilitative context. In terms of client goals, the distinction between process and outcome goals is predicated on the concept of the client's capacity to "live, learn, and work independently." Any goal that directly represents that end may be considered a client outcome goal; other goals that contribute to a client outcome goal are considered client process goals.

For administrative goals, the distinction between process and outcome is based on the concept of the client's capacity to live, learn, and work independently *and* the concept of continued or increased agency funding. Any goal that directly represents independent client functioning or agency funding may be considered an administrative outcome goal; other goals that contribute to an administrative outcome goal are considered process goals. Outcome goals are more important than process goals, and the practitioner will want to consider them as a high priority.

Additional criteria may be used in establishing priorities for the goals. The practitioner may use his or her professional values as a priority criterion. For example, if preventing client rehospitalization were of great importance to the practitioner, such a goal would be considered a higher-priority goal. An additional consideration is the time allotted for the evaluation process. A goal may be prohibitively complex or too large to be evaluated within the allotted span of time.

To determine the highest-priority goals, the practitioner can evaluate each goal from the perspective of each of the aforementioned criteria. The practitioner can determine whether the goal is urgent to the client, the agency, or both; whether it will benefit the client, the agency, or both; whether it is relevant or irrelevant to the practitioner's job description; and whether it is an outcome or a process goal. If a goal is evaluated as urgent to the client and agency, beneficial to the client and the agency, consonant with the practitioner's job description, an outcome goal, and agreeable to the practitioner's professional values, it would emerge as a high-priority goal. Table 8 illustrates a checklist method for determining the highest-priority client and administrative goals. The goals are listed vertically in their respective categories: client goals, administrative goals, joint client and administrative goals. The criteria are listed horizontally. The goals are then checked if they fulfill the criteria (e.g., if they are urgent to the agency or relevant to the practitioner's job description). A practitioner may consider goals with the most check marks as the highest-priority goals.

In Table 8, three goals, "increased number of client-practitioner interviews," "client independent living," and "client job placements" each received five check marks. In such a situation, the practitioner may discriminate among the goals by using such criteria as ease of accomplishing the goal, consideration of time, or ability of the goal to be measured. Note that in Table 8, using these additional criteria, the three highest-priority goals were assigned priorities.

Practice Situations

Using a format similar to Table 8, establish priorities for the client and administrative goals that you listed in your client and administrative goals charts. First, list the client, administrative, and joint goals. Remember not to list goals more than once. Second, evaluate the goals by the previously discussed criteria. Third, check those goals that are urgent, are beneficial, conform to your job description, are outcome goals, and match your professional values. Fourth, numerically assign priority to your highest-priority goals (e.g., those goals with the most check marks).

Having established priorities for the goals, the practitioner is almost ready to begin evaluating his or her performance on these goals. However, because the practitioner has a limited amount of time to devote to evaluating and improving his or her performance, it is necessary to choose the initial goals for evaluation. For the purposes of this book, only the top two goals on the sample priority chart (Table 8) will be considered further. The practitioner can choose from one to all of the goals at the beginning of the evaluation process. The decision is based on the amount of time available for evaluation and improvement activities. Once the practitioner has a clear idea of the goals with which to begin the evaluation process, he or she is ready to begin the second major phase of professional evaluation. The second phase will describe the skills needed to clearly define and measure the practitioner's performance on the goals.

Table 8.   Priority Chart

Goals	Urgency Client	Urgency Agency	Benefit Client	Benefit Agency	Job Description	Outcome Goal	Other: Professional Value	Priorities
Client Goals:								
1. Clients show up for scheduled appointments.	✓	✓	✓	✓				
2. Clients explore problems at personal meaning level.			✓				✓	
3. Clients contact practitioner when there is a crisis.	✓		✓				✓	
4. Clients work to identify skill strengths and deficits.			✓				✓	
5. Clients help to operationally define skill strengths and deficits.			✓					
6. Clients agree to work to reach the skill growth goals defined on their Client Assessment Charts.		✓	✓	✓			✓	
7. Clients help to identify the steps that will lead to achievement of their skill growth goals.			✓				✓	
8. Clients can demonstrate job acquisition skills.	✓		✓				✓	
9. Clients can demonstrate independent living skills.	✓		✓				✓	
10. Clients get positive on-the-job evaluation report from supervisors.	✓		✓			✓	✓	
11. Clients keep job for at least one year.	✓		✓			✓	✓	
12. Clients live independently for at least one year.	✓		✓			✓	✓	

Goals	Urgency		Benefit		Job Description	Outcome Goal	Other: Professional Value	Priorities
	Client	Agency	Client	Agency				
Administrative Goals:								
1. Providing federally mandated services.		✓		✓	✓	✓		
2. Increased number of client interviews.		✓		✓	✓	✓	✓	1
3. Client satisfaction.		✓	✓	✓			✓	
4. Cost efficiency.				✓				
5. Cost effectiveness.				✓				
6. Availability of services.		✓		✓				
7. Relationship with many community resources and potential employers.			✓	✓				
8. Positive community opinion.				✓				
9. Preventing client hospitalizations.			✓	✓		✓	✓	
Joint Client and Administrative Goals:								
1. Client achievement of rehabilitation benefits (maintain job and/or independent living).			✓	✓		✓	✓	
2. Client job placements.	✓		✓	✓	✓	✓		3
3. Helping clients to live independently in the community.	✓		✓	✓	✓	✓		2

ESTABLISHING PRIORITIES FOR THE GOALS: A SUMMARY

Goal: To determine the relative importance of the goals and to select the goals for evaluation

1. Analyze the goals by the criteria of:
   (a) urgency to the client or the agency;
   (b) benefit to the client or the agency;
   (c) conformance with the practitioner's job descriptions;
   (d) classification of the goal as an outcome goal;
   (e) consistency with the practitioner's values.
2. Identify the high priority goals.

SETTING REHABILITATION GOALS: A SKILLED APPROACH

Like Ed, whom we met earlier, Sheila worked as a psychiatric rehabilitation practitioner with an agency committed to meeting the placement needs of its numerous clients. But, unlike Ed, Sheila tried to relate the needs of her clients to the goals of the agency.

When beginning her evaluation, Sheila explored all of the options open to her clients. She realized there were many placement possibilities. Sheila also understood that placement was a means to an end. Her clients had a variety of needs, and each need dictated a unique placement goal. Sheila wanted to place her clients, but she also wanted to make sure that her clients achieved their rehabilitation goals. At the beginning of her evaluation, Sheila made a point of meeting with her supervisor. She outlined her goals and then asked her supervisor to comment on some of the things that might be important from an agency or administrative point of view.

The supervisor looked at Sheila and smiled. Sheila grinned back. "Listen, I know how important the client's needs are, but I want to understand the agency's needs as well. After all, we are both on the same team."

Pleased by this kind of support, the supervisor talked at some length about the various agency goals. What it boiled down to was a series of ways in which the agency necessarily measured its services: the number of clients who could be served by a given workshop without increasing costs; the amount of money that might be realized through sale of the workshop's products in the community at large; and other criteria, most, if not all, dealing with the necessary evil of funds and budgets. Sheila was able to transform most of these concerns into an administrative goal applicable to client needs.

In the end, Sheila had more than half a dozen client and administrative goals of her own. Her next task was to establish priorities for them. In doing so, she used "client urgency or benefit" as her most important criterion, followed closely by "agency urgency or benefit." Her own job responsibilities constituted a third level of significant concern. Last, Sheila determined which goals were outcome goals.

After much effort, Sheila emerged with a list of client and administrative goals for which priorities had been carefully established. In working to achieve these goals, she knew she would simultaneously be meeting the real needs of both her clients and the agency. In reporting on the list to her supervisor, she could hear the gratitude in the other's voice. The supervisor then went on to share a new problem. The supervisor had been worrying about the necessity for all practitioners to see a greater number of clients. Although Sheila herself wanted to be able to spend more time with each client, she would try to think about how she could resolve this problem.

Sheila still wasn't sure how it would turn out. But she knew quite well that the solution she eventually came up with would be a good one.

Chapter 3 MONITORING PERFORMANCE▌

MONITORING PERFORMANCE: AN UNSKILLED APPROACH

Kathy turned her little Volkswagen right onto Maple and caught the next three lights in a row just as they were turning green.

"I must be doing something right," she congratulated herself. And she slowed down to wave at Harv, a fellow practitioner working at Parkwood whose battered Studebaker she spotted just nosing out of a side street.

Poor old Harv. A heck of a nice guy. It was just a shame that he didn't know where he was going with the kids. Pleased with herself and the world in general on the gorgeous May morning, Kathy had plenty of sympathy to spare for Harvey.

It really was a beautiful morning, too. The daffodils and irises planted along the wide median strip were in full bloom. The sky was that absolutely crystal-clear blue associated with spring mornings. And Kathy was looking forward eagerly to the tasks she had set for herself for the day. Today, for the first time as a psychiatric rehabilitation practitioner, she was going to begin evaluating her performance on specific priority goals.

The simple fact that she actually had some goals probably meant she was ahead of the game. Kathy reminded herself of this as she turned right on Federal and then right again into the drive that led to Parkwood School's staff parking lot.

Parkwood was a school for emotionally disturbed adolescents. Kathy was proud of herself for having landed a job there. As her first job following preservice training, the position was a good one. Kathy enjoyed the work. She cared about the kids who were her clients. And she felt sure she was accomplishing something very worthwhile.

Although she didn't yet realize it, Kathy was about to lose some of her easily gained confidence in herself.

All of Kathy's conferences that morning seemed to go well. Ted Jorgenson had apparently been having some problems in one of his classes but with Kathy's help was able to get a handle on them. Alfred Hardin had announced he was on a hunger strike, but Kathy talked with him and got him to agree to go down to lunch with the others in his group. She herself didn't waste much time eating lunch. She was going to start monitoring her work that afternoon, and the prospect excited her.

When the prospect transformed itself into a reality, however, a good deal of Kathy's excitement degenerated into confusion.

She began by looking at the goals she had set — goals that reflected the needs both of her youthful clients and of the institution for which she worked. There were a number of these goals. Kathy arranged them in the order in which she had established priorities for them and began trying to figure out how she was doing. But somehow all of her efforts just seemed to produce more confusion.

She concentrated on one of her highest-priority goals: "to normalize the lives of my clients." She wrestled with her statement of this goal for some time. And it finally dawned upon her that, when all was said and done, she really didn't have a clue as to what this statement meant!

"What it really comes down to is the meaning of 'normalize,'" she told herself. And, of course, she was right. But being right didn't help. Kathy couldn't help feeling, with something very much like despair, that she had left something out in all her careful work up to this point.

Here again, of course, Kathy was quite right. She had neglected to define her goals in any meaningful way — which meant that she really had no way of telling how either a client or she herself was doing.

Kathy never operationalized her goal; she had no idea what actual behavior the goal comprised. As a result, she didn't know whether "normalizing the lives of her clients" meant returning a certain percentage of children to regular school settings or simply reducing by a certain percentage the number of temper flare-ups among her clients — or both. Because she had not operationalized the goal, she had no understanding of what the goal meant in observable and behavioral terms. Moreover, Kathy had failed to determine whether she would need to achieve any prior goals be-

fore she could monitor her performance on the priority goal. These omissions prevented Kathy from conducting her evaluation in any systematic fashion. She had no system for keeping track of the number of temper flare-ups among her clients, for example, because she had never pinpointed such flare-ups as criteria that would require monitoring.

In the end, all Kathy could tell herself was, "I'm helping to normalize the lives of these kids — I think." Somehow the effect of this statement was not very reassuring.

At this point the practitioner has (1) developed a list of client and administrative goals; (2) established priorities for these goals; and (3) selected the high-priority goals for evaluation. This chapter will present the skills practitioners need to evaluate their performance on the high-priority goals. This strategy involves three major skills: (1) setting the intermediary goals related to the high-priority goals; (2) operationalizing the high-priority goals and the related intermediary goals; and (3) developing and implementing a plan to monitor performance on the goals.

IDENTIFYING RELATED INTERMEDIARY GOALS

Before evaluating performance on the priority goals, the practitioner needs to identify the intermediary goals needed to achieve these priority goals. Intermediary goals are the steps that lead to the accomplishment of client or administrative high-priority goals. Determining the related intermediary goals is important for three reasons: (1) the priority goal may be so large or complex that, to be properly evaluated, it would need to be broken down into related and constituent goals; (2) clearly defining and monitoring intermediary goals increases the likelihood that the priority goals will be reached (Hart, 1978); and (3) before monitoring his or her performance on the priority goal, the practitioner may need to ensure that he or she can effectively perform the related and integral subgoals. In other words, the practitioner may not be in a position to evaluate and improve his or her performance on the priority goals without first evaluating and improving performance on the related intermediary goals. For example, the practitioner cannot evaluate and improve performance on the goal of "helping clients to achieve their rehabilitation goals" if the practitioner is not satisfactorily doing the intermediary step of "setting rehabilitation goals." Evaluation and improvement of the primary goal are possible only if the practitioner can improve his or her performance on the related intermediary goals. In most cases, the practitioner will need to also evaluate her or his performance on the related intermediary goals.

For example, suppose a practitioner's second-highest-priority goal was "increasing the number of clients interviewed weekly." In order to determine the intermediary goals, the following question is asked: "What are the steps that lead to being able to serve an increased number of clients?" By consulting supervisors, reading appropriate literature, and using judgment and professional experience, the practitioner can identify several things that need to be done to serve more clients. A sample list includes:

1. Increasing the number of clients the practitioner schedules
2. Reducing client cancelations
3. Reducing client no-shows
4. Increasing the number of clients with mutually agreed-upon skill goals
5. Increasing the number of clients with high-level rehabilitation programs

Each of these steps becomes an intermediary goal that leads to the achievement of the priority goal of "increasing the number of clients interviewed weekly." Having determined the intermediary goals, the practitioner will want to arrange them developmentally — that is, sequence the goals in the order in which they need to be accomplished. To determine the sequence, the practitioner may use his or her own judgment, consult supervisors, or read appropriate literature. Table 9 outlines a list of intermediary goals for selected priority goals.

Table 9.   Intermediary Goals for Priority Goals

I. NUMBER OF CLIENTS INTERVIEWED

    A.   Quantity of clients scheduled

    B.   Quantity of client no-shows

    C.   Quantity of client cancellations

II. CLIENT INDEPENDENT LIVING

    A.   Client level of involvement

    B.   Accuracy of diagnosis

    C.   Client acquisition and application of needed independent living skills

Practice Situations

Practice listing intermediary goals that lead to priority goals. Using a format similar to Table 10, developmentally list at least three intermediary goals for each of the priority goals you have previously identified. Remember to ask the question: "What are the steps that lead to being able to accomplish the priority goal?"

Table 10.   Sample Format for Listing Intermediary Goals for Priority Goals

I.

    A.

    B.

    C.

II.

    A.

    B.

    C.

III.

    A.

    B.

    C.

IDENTIFYING INTERMEDIARY GOALS:
A SUMMARY

Goal: To determine the subgoals that, if achieved, contribute to the practitioner's performance on the high-priority goals

1. Ask self: What are the steps that might lead to the achievement of each high priority goal?
2. Identify those steps as intermediary goals.
3. Sequence these intermediary goals in the approximate order in which they need to be accomplished.

OPERATIONALIZING THE GOALS

The next major step in professional evaluation is to make the priority goals and the intermediary goals capable of evaluation. Often, goals are expressed in abstract and nonspecific terms and thus are not capable of being monitored (e.g., client satisfaction, practitioner work level). The process by which a goal is rendered capable of evaluation is called *operationalizing*. This process is accomplished by specifying the observable behavioral components of the goal and determining how the behavior can be monitored. For example, the priority goal of "preventing client hospitalization" might be operationalized to "the percentage of clients who are still living outside a hospital one year after termination of the rehabilitation process." In other words, the goal has been transformed (operationalized) into observable and measurable terms, and the practitioner can monitor his or her performance on the goal. Often, the priority and intermediary goals may already be partially operationalized (e.g., "increased number of client-practitioner interviews").

A number of research articles appearing in a variety of professional journals have verified that operationalizing goals can have a positive impact on outcome. Smith (1976) has reported research indicating that simply requiring a counselor or therapist to set observable goals seems to improve therapeutic outcome in and of itself. In areas as diverse as the world of work, conservation programming, and social-skills training, goal-setting interventions have been effectively used to increase performance (Bucker, 1978; Erez, 1977; Flowers, 1978; Latham and Rinne, 1974). Administrative decision making has also been found to be improved through the operationalization of goals (Alden, 1978).

In cases where the priority or intermediary goal has not been adequately operationalized (e.g., client satisfaction), the practitioner will need to define exactly what behavior is going to be evaluated. The procedure used to operationalize goals is similar to the rehabilitation assessment skill the practitioner uses to operationalize client skills (Book 1: *The Skills of Diagnostic Planning*). Specifically, this procedure involves writing a statement that answers the following questions:

1. Who is to perform the behavior (the client or the practitioner)?
2. What is the name of the behavior to be performed (goal)?
3. What are the observable behavioral components (e.g., tasks or observable actions)?
4. How is the behavior to be measured (e.g., number, levels, amounts, frequency, or percentage of incidence)?
5. When and where is the observable behavior to be performed (e.g., specific situations or places)?

By indicating these specific details for each goal, the rehabilitation practitioner has clearly defined the goal and can then monitor and evaluate his or her performance on the goal.

For example, the goal of "practitioner work level" could be defined thus:

Who?	The practitioner
What goal?	Work level
What behavior?	Clients interviewed individually or in groups by the practitioner
How measured?	Number
When/where?	In a week at rehabilitation agency

Having answered the appropriate questions, the practitioner can evaluate his or her performance. For example, "practitioner work level" has been defined as "the number of clients interviewed individually or in groups by the practitioner in a week at the rehabilitation agency." Of course, practitioner work level might be defined differently by another practitioner. When operationalizing the goal, the practitioner may also find that the goal contains more than one behavioral component. For example, "practitioner work level" might also be defined as "the number of hours of rehabilitation contact with clients in a week." The practitioner may therefore want to evaluate his or her performance on both "number of clients interviewed weekly" and "number of weekly client contact hours." Table 11 is an example of two priority goals and their related intermediary goals, which have been operationalized.

The key to determining whether a goal is fully operationalized is to make sure that the observable behaviors are identified, that the time and the place they are to be performed is clarified, and that the measurement technique is specified.

Practice Situations

Practice operationalizing goals by operationalizing the goal of client satisfaction and the intermediary goals used as examples in Table 11. Complete a chart similar to Table 12 for your three highest-priority goals and the three related intermediary goals you listed in Table 10. You can obtain additional practice in operationalizing goals by operationalizing other goals you listed previously.

Table 11. Operationalized Goals Chart

Goals	Operationalized Goals
I. Number of clients interviewed	I. The number of clients interviewed by the practitioner during a week at the rehabilitation agency
A. Quantity of clients scheduled	A. The number of clients scheduled for interviews with the practitioner in a week at the rehabilitation agency.
B. Quantity of client cancellations	B. The number of clients each week who cancel an appointment with the practitioner
C. Quantity of client no-shows	C. The number of clients each week who fail to show up for or cancel an appointment with the practitioner
II. Client independent living	II. The percentage of clients who, within 25 sessions, achieve independent living goals written in client files
A. Client level of involvement	A. The percentage of clients whose average involvement is level 4 or greater, as measured by the client involvement scale during the first five sessions with the practitioner
B. Accuracy of diagnosis	B. The percentage of clients who have accurate independent living skills diagnoses as determined by mutually agreed-upon present level of skill functioning written on signed client assessment chart in client file
C. Client acquisition and application of needed independent living skills	C. The percentage of clients who have at least four independent living skills acquisition and/or application programs in their files as measured by the program development scales

Table 12. Practice Operationalized Goals Chart

Goals	Operationalized Goals
Goal I.	I.
Intermediary A.	A.
Intermediary B.	B.
Intermediary C.	C.
Goal II.	II.
Intermediary A.	A.
Intermediary B.	B.
Intermediary C.	C.
Goal III.	III.
Intermediary A.	A.
Intermediary B.	B.
Intermediary C.	C.

OPERATIONALIZING THE GOALS: A SUMMARY

Goal: To make the priority and intermediary goals capable of evaluation

1. Specify whether the client or the practitioner is to perform the behavior.
2. Specify the name of the behavior to be performed.
3. Specify the tasks or observable behaviors.
4. Specify how the behavior is to be measured.
5. Specify when and where the behavior is to be performed.

DEVELOPING AND IMPLEMENTING A MONITORING PLAN

The final step in monitoring the practitioner's performance on the goals is to develop and implement a monitoring plan. The plan includes specific methods for monitoring performance on the intermediary and priority goals. The plan should answer the following questions:

1. Whose behavior is to be monitored? (Name person whose behavior is monitored.)
2. Who is to do the monitoring? (Name person who will do the monitoring.)
3. How is the monitoring to be done? (Specify monitoring device.)
4. When is the monitoring to be done? (Specify appropriate time and dates.)
5. Where is the monitoring to be done? (Specify place where monitoring occurs.)

Table 13 presents a monitoring plan for the practitioner's performance on the goal, "clients interviewed weekly."

Table 13. Monitoring Plan for Goal of "Increased Number of Clients Interviews"

Operationalized goal: The number of clients interviewed by the practitioner during a week at the rehabilitation agency

1. Whose behavior is to be monitored?
   Practitioner's

2. Who does the monitoring?
   Receptionist

3. How is the monitoring to be done?
   Record-keeping: When the practitioner interviews a client, the receptionist puts a check mark next to the client's name in agency schedule book. Receptionist records weekly totals and gives to the practitioner.

4. When is the monitoring to be done?
   At the beginning of the interview

5. Where is the monitoring to be done?
   Reception area of rehabilitation agency

The specification of whose behavior is to be monitored flows from the operationalized goal. In the majority of cases, either the client's or the practitioner's behavior will be monitored. The decision about who is to monitor is more complicated. The practitioner, a supervisor, clerical staff, or even the client may be appropriate choices. In some cases, significant others or community resources' staff will be in the best position to monitor the behavior. The factors in determining the best person to do the monitoring can include the ability to monitor accurately, accessibility to the behavior being monitored, and sufficient time to monitor. At times, the practitioner and others can monitor equally. The decision then may be based on practical (e.g., time, cost) or political (e.g., believability) factors. For example, both the practitioner and the agency receptionist may be capable of monitoring the number of clients the practitioner interviews weekly at the rehabilitation center. The practitioner may choose the receptionist as the person to do the monitoring, basing the decision on political (believability) and practical (time) considerations. The persons doing the monitoring may vary as goals vary, but all results are reported to the person responsible for the evaluation (i.e., the practitioner or his or her designee).

The most difficult decision involves determining how the monitoring can best be done. Many monitoring alternatives exist, and practitioners will want to be familiar with the different options available in a particular rehabilitation setting. One way to review such options is to consider them in terms of three distinct modes of data collection: (1) *self-report;* (2) *direction observation* by others; and (3) *indirect methods.* Each of these basic modes entails a variety of options or strategies.

Monitoring based upon *self-report* without the use of video technology requires a client or practitioner to keep continuous track of what is done in a given period of activity. This monitoring mode is sometimes known as "process recording."

Since monitoring assumes that data are retained long enough to allow evaluation, the client or practitioner would have to either maintain a written record during the period of activity or remember the relevant data for later consideration. Both procedures entail obvious problems in any kind of complex skill-related activity. In an interview with a client, for example, a practitioner will invariably need to concentrate all available energy on performance rather than on retention. In addition, there is the danger of distortion in self-recall. In complex activities, self-report may provide essential information about overall feelings, impressions, and the like. This information can be complemented by and compared to data obtained through some more objective monitoring technique. Following simulated job interviews, for example, clients can comment on positive and negative aspects of their performance as perceived during the interaction. The "interviewers" can also become involved in the monitoring process by commenting on their own physical, cognitive, and affective states during the interview.

With the help of video technology, practitioners and clients can learn to observe their own videotaped interviews with or without the use of a skills checklist. In the first stage of such monitoring activities, the practitioner or client can review the tape independently and then compare and discuss the ratings with others (e.g., supervisor or colleague) who have done the same. Such an effort is valuable if self-assessment skills are to be developed. In this way, self-report skills themselves can be monitored and developed. Practitioners may want to include a self-report component in any monitoring system utilized.

Direct observation is an obvious and extremely useful monitoring strategy that entails a number of different options. The practitioner can observe a client or clients involved in a given skill-related activity.

There are a number of ways in which direct, live observation can be employed as a monitoring strategy. In a simulated client-placement interview that takes place in the practitioner's presence, for example, the practitioner may simply sit and watch. In an actual placement interview (e.g., noncompetitive employment placement), the practitioner may obtain the client's permission to sit in and watch the proceedings; or, again with the client's permission (and assuming an appropriate setting), the practitioner may observe the interview through a one-way mirror. The practitioner may also arrange for a supervisor or colleague to observe his or her behavior with clients.

As with self-report, direct observation requires the retention of relevant data for subsequent evaluation. Since an "outside" observer presumably will have no duties other than monitoring, there is no reason he or she cannot keep a continuous written record of the important data or use some form of checklist. Indeed, the use of a predesigned checklist is highly recommended.

Direct observation can be enhanced by the use of both audiotape and videotape recordings. An audio recorder can be helpful in monitoring aspects of a client's interpersonal skills, such as content of speech and tone of voice or aspects of the practitioner's interviewing skills, such as responding skills. If the practitioner wanted to ascertain the number of times a client addressed a real or role-played acquaintance by name, or to study a client's voice tone with an angry parent, for example, an audio recording would serve the purpose well. A videotape recording of the interaction would serve equally well here, assuming it was equipped with a sound track. In addition, of course, a video recording would allow the gathering of a wide range of nonverbal data as well (e.g., practitioner's or client's behavioral communication of interest).

The virtue of any mechanical recording is that it provides practitioner and client with a permanent and faithful record of what occurred. This record can then be reviewed and evaluated many times.

There are some problems with mechanical recording. Video recordings involve a special set-up effort; they are sometimes expensive; and they can be somewhat intrusive.

Finally, there are *indirect methods* (e.g., client file audits, record keeping) of monitoring client or practitioner behavior. They tend to be inexpensive and efficient, especially when one is dealing with large groups. Client file audits and record keeping can monitor competence in information gathering and can also be used as a check for the use of certain procedures (e.g., goal setting).

Deciding *how to monitor* involves selection from the alternative techniques (self-report, direct observation, indirect methods). The technique selected will depend primarily on the appropriateness of the technique to the goal. Other important considerations will include the reliability, validity, availability, time, and cost of the alternative techniques. Once the technique has been selected, the monitoring instruments can be acquired or designed (e.g., checklists, questionnaires, record-keeping forms).

The next decision to be made is when to monitor. The broadest time categories are before, during, and after rehabilitation services have been received by the client. Using these categories, the practitioner can specify the appropriate time and dates for monitoring (e.g., before, during, at the end of a course on job-interviewing skills, and six months after the course). Monitoring at the end of the rehabilitation process can be used to assess the progress that has taken place. "Follow-up monitoring" can be used to assess how much progress is retained. For example, for the monitoring of "client satisfaction," a follow-up questionnaire might be sent out to a sample of the clients of the practitioner, after the initial interview, at the end of the rehabilitation process, and six months after termination of services.

An additional consideration is the length of time needed to monitor. The amount of time necessary for a direct observation, videotaped recording, or written sample of a behavior needs to be specified. In addition, the determination of what is a sufficient amount of time may be predetermined by the monitoring device, logistic constraints, opportunities to repeat the monitoring, reviews of the research literature, or the practitioner's definition of acceptable reliability.

The specification of where the monitoring takes place will flow from the goal and the monitoring device. For example, "client problem exploration as measured by audiotape ratings using the client process scale" would probably be done in the office of the rehabilitation practitioner.

After developing a plan for monitoring the operationalized goal, the practitioner needs an appropriate way to accumulate the monitoring results. The first decision the practitioner needs to make is whether the results will be kept by hand or by computer. Of course, the decision to use a computerized data-processing system will depend on the availability of such a system within the rehabilitation agency. If the results are to be stored by hand, the practitioner will need to design forms that will store the information simply. These forms may be kept by the practitioner or by the clerical staff, depending on the resources of the rehabilitation agency. Table 14 provides the form developed to keep the results of the monitoring of the practitioner's performance on the goal, "clients interviewed weekly." The form also includes space for storage of additional information. Another decision must be made as to how often the results are to be totaled or averaged. Determining monthly averages that can be viewed quarterly, semi-annually, and annually is most practical. These averages can provide the practitioner with both immediate learning and easy access to the information needed for more global learning about his or her performance.

Table 14. Record-Keeping Form for "Number of Client Interviews" Results

Week	Number of Clients Scheduled	Number of Clients Interviewed	Number of Client Cancelations	Number of Client No-Show	Number of Client Contact Hours	Total Case Load	Percentage of Case Load Seen
Totals for month of March							
Average for month of March							
Totals for month of April							
Average for month of April							
Totals for month of May							
Average for month of May							

Practice Situations

Practice developing a monitoring plan. First, using the space provided in Table 15, develop the plan to monitor the practitioner's performance on the goal of "client satisfaction." Second, practice by developing a monitoring plan for one of the five goals with which you have been working (i.e., one you have already operationalized). Then practice designing forms to retain the monitoring data. Design a form for recording the results of the practitioner's performance on the goal, "client satisfaction" and design a form for recording the results to be gathered from the implementation of your monitoring of the goal for which you developed a monitoring plan. Practice carrying out the monitoring plan for the goal for which you have designed a record-keeping form. Complete the form, based on the results of your monitoring. Once you have developed and implemented your monitoring plan, you are ready to learn from the results and develop new direction for improving your performance.

Table 15. Sample Format for Developing A Monitoring Plan for the Goal of "Client Satisfaction"

Operationalized goal: The percentage of clients who indicate an average of 3.5 or more on client satisfaction follow-up questionnaire

1. Whose behavior is to be monitored?
2. Who does the monitoring?
3. How is the monitoring to be done?
4. When is the monitoring to be done?
5. Where is the monitoring to be done?

DEVELOPING AND IMPLEMENTING A MONITORING PLAN: A SUMMARY

Goal: To monitor the practitioner's performance on the operationalized goal

1. Specify the person whose behavior is to be monitored.

2. Specify the person who is to do the monitoring.

3. Specify the monitoring device.

4. Specify the appropriate time and dates for the monitoring.

5. Specify where the monitoring is to occur.

6. Determine how the monitoring results will be retained (in written form or by computer).

MONITORING PERFORMANCE: A SKILLED APPROACH

"How's it going, Rick?" Marge, Rick's supervisor at Mercy Hospital's special predischarge ward, stood in the open doorway and regarded him cheerfully.

Rick grinned at her. "Maybe you don't want to ask that question too lightly," he cautioned her. "I'm finishing up doing a six-month self-evaluation. If you really want to know, I can share with you what I've been doing."

"Really?" Marge looked both skeptical and intrigued at once. She moved into the room and sat down. "Well give, give! I'm all ears."

"You asked for it!" Rick shuffled though some papers and came up with the one he wanted. He began by outlining his original client and administrative goals and explaining the way in which he had assigned priorities to them. Marge was already familiar with several of the goals that related to the hospital's own needs; she'd talked with Rick about them some months ago.

"It was a struggle just to establish priorities effectively," Rick told her. "And then, once I had established priorities, I realized that each was a major task in itself. I mean, the whole idea of setting a goal with clients that in-

volves their making a 'satisfactory adjustment to home life' is a biggie."

"So?" Marge was watching Rick closely.

"So I did a couple of things. First, I worked to set related intermediary goals — things that I needed to do to reach my priority goals. For example, one intermediary goal I set up for the 'satisfactory-adjustment-at-home' goal was to help clients learn to relate to their families. At the same time, I worked to state each priority intermediary goal in really concrete, meaningful terms."

"You clearly defined your goals," Marge volunteered, her eyes still on him.

"Uh-huh — which meant really pinning down and defining exactly what I meant at every point."

By now Rick was caught up in his explanation. "When it came to monitoring the goal of 'satisfactory adjustment,' I decided to use a self-report-after-six-months method. So over the last couple of weeks I visited each of my people at home and talked with them about the kind of adjustment they had made."

"Sounds great," Marge told him. "But let's go back to that self-report business for a minute. When you visited their homes, what did you do — just talk with each person?"

Rick shook his head vigorously. "Uh-huh — I made up a simple questionnaire. That way it was easier for them to give specific answers — and also easier for me to deal with the results. I have the completed questionnaires, but I haven't gotten around to organizing them yet. But they look positive." He grabbed a heap of papers. "Here, you want to take a look?"

Marge got up grinning. "I'd like to a little later. Right now, though, I'm running behind — and I'm going to have to catch up with my schedule."

She turned to leave. But in the doorway, she turned back and looked at Rick once more.

"I think what you've done is fantastic. Thanks." And she was gone.

Chapter 4 DEVELOPING NEW DIRECTION

DEVELOPING NEW DIRECTION: AN UNSKILLED APPROACH

The Mohawk Clinic was a drug rehabilitation facility committed to vocationally training and placing its clients. Since coming to the clinic, David had seen its high rate of success, and he strived to maintain this standard. To that end, he had recently conducted an evaluation of his performance in helping clients to complete their vocational training.

One day, at lunch, Peg, a fellow practitioner, said to him, "You look kind of depressed today. What's the matter?"

*"You know that this clinic is one of the most successful drug rehabilitation facilities in the state. I just conducted an evaluation to determine the percentage of **my** clients who completed vocational training programs."*

"That sounds ambitious," Peg volunteered.

"Yes, but unfortunately only forty-six percent of my clients completed their training programs this year." Idly twisting his fork in his hand, David continued, "It seems so fruitless. I realized the goals of our clients and the criteria for the clinic's funding are virtually identical — that is, vocational placement. I set all the related intermediary goals I needed to perform to be sure I could achieve the priority goal. I operationalized my goals, developed a monitoring plan with other institutions to keep track of my clients' progress, and recorded all the information on forms. Just to find out that I'm not doing very well." The fork fell from his hand and struck the plate with a bang, scattering the uneaten peas.

Peg looked at him quizzically. "David, I'm surprised at you. You didn't expect to find yourself one hundred percent, or even eighty percent successful, did you? Didn't you have a reason, a purpose for the evaluation?"

"What do you mean?" David asked.

"Well — it seems to me that your purpose is to improve your performance. Now, you have all this data that — al-

though it shows you aren't glaringly successful — can be used to improve your work. You're ahead of the game in having all these results. Don't lose your confidence now."

David squinted at her. Then, musing, he said, "I think you're right. Somewhere in all the data are indications as to how I can improve my performance."

Peg nodded her head in agreement.

"What do I owe you for your insight?" David asked.

"Just show me how you did your evaluation," Peg answered.

Once the practitioner has understood his or her performance on the goal, he or she will want to organize and use the results of the evaluation. Evaluation results will be most useful when they are organized in an understandable manner. The first step is to develop a scale to organize the results. The second step is to develop and implement a plan for using the results. The third step is to recycle the evaluation process itself by evaluating other high-priority goals. Rehabilitation practitioners who evaluate their performance will be constantly improving as results lead to new directions that improve their delivery of rehabilitation services.

DEVELOPING A SCALE TO ORGANIZE THE RESULTS

After the evaluation record-keeping forms have been completed, the practitioner needs a way to organize the results of the evaluation. To be used most effectively, the results need to be functionally or understandably organized.

The first step is to develop scales for each operationalized goal, designating five levels of achievement. In order to develop the scales, the practitioner explores three questions:

1. What amount of the goal would be considered optimum?

2. What amount of the goal would be considered average?

3. What amount of the goal would be considered undesirable?

The first question addresses level 5 of the projected scale, the second question addresses level 3, and the third question addresses level 1. Levels 2 and 4 simply fill in the space between the other levels.

There are a number of ways to determine the five levels of achievement of a goal: practitioner judgment, knowledge of the literature, administrative demands, or analyzing present performance and then setting levels based on the belief that present performance is average. In actual practice, the levels are typically set by the practitioner prior to collection of the evaluative data. However, the levels of the scale may be changed at any time, based on the learning obtained from the evaluation.

An example of a scale for practitioner "contacts with community resources" might be:

Level 5: More than six community resources toured monthly

Level 4: Four to six community resources toured monthly

Level 3: Two to three community resources toured monthly

Level 2: One community resource toured monthly

Level 1: No community resources toured monthly

Scales help the practitioner to understand each goal in enough detail that his or her performance can be evaluated. The specific quantities of each level should be based on the practitioner's situation (e.g., administrative demands, setting, case load, client populations). The specific levels used in this chapter are given primarily as an example of the evaluation process and may not be applicable to any particular practitioner's situation.

Several other aspects of the scales need to be mentioned. First, as indicated in the "contacts with community resources" example, the various points on the scale do not have to refer to a single quantity. Rather, the reference points can contain a range of items (e.g., two to three community resources). Second, such ranges do not have to be the same size. Again, this is illustrated in the previous example: level 4 specifies a range of three resources per week, although level 3 specifies a range of only two resources. Third, all points on the scale do not have to be filled in. This is often the case where five different quantities of the variable are not really functional. At the extreme, there may be only two points. For example, suppose the practitioner operationalized a goal as "the number of clients requesting transfer to a new practitioner in six months' time." The practitioner might determine that it is undesirable to have even a single request for a transfer to a new practitioner. The scale might then look like this:

Level 5:

Level 4:

Level 3: No requests for transfer

Level 2:

Level 1: One or more requests for transfer

The scales should ultimately reflect the functional differences in the practitioner's performance on the goal. In this regard, it is important that the practitioner understand the rationale for each point on the scale.

Table 16 presents examples of scales for four different operationalized goals. The levels were determined through a combination of the practitioner's judgment, administrative demands, and knowledge of the literature.

Table 16. Scales for Operationalized Goals

Goal	Operationalized Goal	Rationale	Level	Scale
Number of clients interviewed	The number of clients interviewed by the practitioner during a week at the rehabilitation agency	Administrative demand	5 4 3 2 1	30 or more 23–29 18–22 10–17 0–9
Quantity of client no-shows	The number of clients each week who don't show up for or cancel an appointment with the practitioner	Practitioner judgement and literature	5 4 3 2 1	 0 1 2 or more
Client independent living	The percentage of clients who, within 25 sessions, achieve the independent living goals written in the client files	Practitioner judgement and administrative demand	5 4 3 2 1	80–100 66–79 65 50–64 0–49
Accuracy of diagnosis	The percentage of clients who have accurate independent living skills diagnoses as determined by mutually agreed-upon present level of skill functioning written on signed client assessment chart in client file	Practitioner judgement	5 4 3 2 1	 100 50 25

Practice Situations

Practice developing scales for operationalized goals. First, using a format similar to Table 16, develop a scale for the "client satisfaction" goal you previously operationalized. Indicate the rationale that you use to determine the varying levels of the scale. Second, using a format similar to Table 16, develop scales for one of the high priority and related intermediary goals that you previously operationalized in Table 12. Next to each scale, indicate the rationale used to determine the varying levels of the scale.

DEVELOPING A SCALE TO ORGANIZE THE RESULTS: A SUMMARY

Goal: To give meaning to the practitioner's performance on the goal

1. Determine the scale levels prior to completing the evaluation process.
2. Designate five levels of achievement of the goal (e.g., optimum, average, undersirable).
3. Be sure to understand the rationale for the identification of the specific scale points (e.g., professional judgment, administrative demands).
4. Change the levels of the scale at any time, based on learning obtained from the evaluation process.

DEVELOPING AND IMPLEMENTING A PLAN TO USE THE RESULTS

Developing a scale to organize the evaluation results will give the practitioner a clear picture of his or her performance in relation to the previously identified standard. Now, the practitioner will want to develop and implement a plan to effectively use the results.

A plan for using the evaluation results is essential. The practitioner carried out the evaluation to ultimately improve his or her performance with clients or, in some cases, to meet administrative demands, and/or possibly to develop his or her own career. The plan to use the evaluation results reflects these initial objectives. Table 17 illustrates a completed record-keeping form for the goal of "number of client interviews" — operationalized as "the number of clients interviewed by the practitioner during a week at the rehabilitation agency." Table 18 portrays the practitioner's raw and scaled scores for that goal as well as the raw and scaled scores for the related intermediary goals. Based on these data, the plan to use the results will be developed.

Table 17. Completed Record-Keeping Form for "Number of Client Interviews" Results

Week	Number of Clients Scheduled	Number of Clients Interviewed	Number of Client Cancellations	Number of Client No-Shows	Number of Client Contact Hours	Total Case Load	Percentage of Case Load Interviewed
2/28–3/4	23	18	2	3	18	60	30
3-7–3/11	24	19	3	2	19	64	29
3/14–3/18	25	17	2	3	18	62	27
3/21–3/25	20	15	2	3	17	60	25
3/28–4/1	18	16	1	1	18	58	27
Totals for month of March	110	85	10	12	90	304	138
Average for month of March	22	17	2	2.4	18	61	28
4/4–4/8	20	17	2	1	18	62	27
4/11–4/15	20	15	3	2	15	62	24
4/18–4/22	22	14	4	3	15	64	22
4/25–4/29	20	18	1	1	20	62	28
Totals for month of April	82	64	10	7	68	250	101
Average for month of April	20.5	16	2.5	1.7	17	62.5	25
5/2–5/6	20	16	2	2	16	62	26
5/9–5/13	19	14	3	2	15	60	23
5/16–5/20	19	15	2	2	17	58	26
5/23–5/27	18	15	1	2	16	60	25
Totals for month of May	76	60	8	8	64	240	100
Average for month of May	19	15	2	2	16	60	25
3-month average	20.5	16	2.2	2	17	61.2	26

Table 18. Scaled Scores for "Number of Client Interviews" Goals and Related Intermediary Goals

Goal	Operationalized Goal	Scale	Results
I. Number of Client Interviews	The number of clients interviewed by the practitioner during a week at the rehabilitation agency	5 = 30 or more 4 = 23 – 29 3 = 18 – 22 2 = 10 – 17 1 = 0 – 9	16 (level 2)

Intermediary Goals

Goal	Operationalized Goal	Scale	Results
A. Quantity of Clients Scheduled	The number of clients scheduled for interviews with the practitioner in a week at the rehabilitation agency	5 = 31 or more 4 = 24 – 30 3 = 19 – 24 2 = 15 – 18 1 = below 15	20 (level 3)
B. Quantity of Client Cancellations	The number of clients each week who cancel an appointment with the practitioner	5 = 0 4 = 1 3 = 2 – 3 2 = 4 – 5 1 = above 6	2.2 (level 3)
C. Quantity of Client No-Shows	The number of clients each week who don't show up for or cancel an appointment with the practitioner	5 4 3 = 0 2 = 1 1 = 2 or more	2 (level 1)

Practitioners must often undertake an evaluation to obtain some information as to how well they are performing in some aspect of their job so that, if necessary, they can improve their efforts. Thus, if the practitioner is not pleased with the evaluation results, she or he will usually want to find a way to improve her or his performance.

Essentially, there are two major ways to improve performance on a particular goal: (1) making the goal observable (i.e., operationalizing the goal); and (2) identifying the specific steps needed to improve performance on the goal.

The first major method, making the goal observable, has, of course, already occurred as a step in the evaluation process. It is documented that performance toward a particular goal can be positively affected simply by objectively identifying the particular goals toward which the person will work. Thus, an important benefit of the professional evaluation process is that the practitioner may improve performance as a function of simply operationalizing goals. That is, the practitioner's knowledge of his or her performance in relation to what is *objectively* desired or expected can, in and of itself, improve performance.

The value of operationalizing goals is not just in having a clear target for which to aim. Observable goals also facilitate the provision of more accurate learning about performance. Knowledge about the practitioner's effectiveness in achieving observable goals can also positively impact the practitioner's rehabilitation outcome. For example, Walker (1972) found that, when opportunities for rehabilitation practitioners learning about how well their clients were achieving rehabilitation goals was experimentally withdrawn, the number of client rehabilitated decreased; likewise, when the practitioners were once again provided information as to how well their clients were achieving their goals, the rehabilitation outcome improved.

However, for some practitioners, the operationalization of their goals and the knowledge of their performance in relation to these observable goals are not in and of themselves enough to improve their performances. These practitioners need to also use the other major method of achieving an evaluation goal: developing and implementing a program of steps necessary to attain the goal.

In order to develop such a program, the practitioner uses much the same skills she or he would use to develop a program for a client. In this instance, however, the practitioner is developing the program to improve her or his own performance rather than the skills of the clients. These program development skills are presented in Book 2 of this series (*The Skills of Rehabilitation Programming*) and thus will not be elaborated on in this book. However, several programming points need to be made that are specific to the skills of professional evaluation.

In developing programs capable of improving performance on a high-priority goal, the practitioner will want to improve performance on any related intermediary goals that are not being performed satisfactorily. In this way, the practitioner's performance on both the high-priority goal and the intermediary goals can be improved.

For example, reexamine Table 18, which illustrates the scaled scores for the goal of "number of client interviews." Note that this goal probably could be achieved by increasing the practitioner's performance on any of the related intermediary goals, that is, by scheduling more clients, by reducing client cancelations, and by decreasing the number of client no-shows. However, only on the goal of decreasing client no-shows has the practitioner rated at less than a satisfactory level. On the other two intermediary goals, the practitioner's scaled scores indicate at least satisfactory performance. In other words, the practitioner seems to be scheduling enough weekly interviews and has an average level of client cancelations. Thus, it would make sense for this practitioner to try and achieve the priority goal of increasing the number of clients interviewed weekly by working toward the intermediary goal of reducing the number of no-shows. Therefore, the practitioner's program goal is to improve his or her ability to reduce no-shows (from a scale score of level 1 to a scale score of level 3). Level 3 performance (zero no-shows per week) becomes the observable goal toward which the practitioner will develop the program.

At its most fundamental level, program development involves brainstorming and sequencing the behavioral steps necessary to advance from a present level of functioning to a needed level of functioning (Anthony, 1979). In this example, the practitioner will have to develop and sequence the behavioral steps necessary to reduce the practitioner's typical number of weekly no-shows from two to zero. Table 19 is an example of program steps for reducing "no-shows." It may well be that this program will also be helpful in reducing the number of client cancelations.

Table 19. An Evaluation Program

Operationalized Goal: To reduce the weekly number of client no-shows from two to zero

Time Line	*Major and Secondary Steps*
May 20	1. Obtain permission of supervisor to institute no-show plan.
May 22	2. Arrange for receptionist to phone each client one day before scheduled appointment and to mail out appointment reminders one week before scheduled appointment. a. Revise receptionist's work schedule to allow time for these activities.
May 29	3. Type and copy appointment reminders. a. Collect sample appointment reminders used by other professionals. b. Write up own appointment reminders.
June 7	4. Receptionist begins to mail out appointment reminders weekly. a. Practitioner signs each reminder before mailing.
June 10	5. Receptionist begins calling clients one day prior to scheduled appointment.

A general principle in writing programs is that a good program is as simple and brief as possible. When the goal has been observably defined, practitioners will always be able to obtain feedback as to whether or not the particular program has been successful. If the program has not been effective in reaching the evaluation goal, modifications will, of course, have to be made. Practitioners will often want to use colleagues who have documented success in achieving the particular evaluation goal to help them brainstorm and sequence some of the steps.

In developing a program to reach the evaluation goal, the practitioner and any colleagues who might be assisting first brainstorm the steps involved in reaching the goal. Second, they sequence or order the steps, in terms of which step is completed first, second, third, and so on. Next, they develop the intermediary or secondary steps that lead to the major steps. This last process is necessary only if the practitioner believes he or she needs more detail to accomplish the major steps. The practitioner looks at the program steps and determines whether he or she can say, "I know how to do each of these steps." Depending on whether or not the practitoners can say this, the program can range from a simple outline of what is to be done to a highly detailed program.

In addition to developing the program steps, the practitioner needs to consider several other points that will be helpful in the implementation of the program. The practitioner can develop time lines for each of the major steps. These time lines, or time limits, can serve to keep the practitioner on track, can give the practitioner a target to aim for, and can become part of the criteria on which the practitioner can evaluate performance and administer differential reinforcements.

The idea of administering differential reinforcements to oneself based on improvement (or lack thereof) is often overlooked, or seen as "unprofessional." Simply achieving the goal of the program is viewed as sufficient reward. Yet simple reinforcements that can be self-administered sometimes make the extra effort that goes into implementing the program seem more enjoyable. The practitioner may wish to give him/herself a small reward after a certain number of major steps are completed (e.g., a sundae, an extra session of racquet ball, a new book, a movie) or a larger reward after the goal is achieved (e.g., going out to dinner, going on a ski weekend, attending an all-day conference). Rewards not only are appropriate but also facilitate the performance of the practitioner's program.

As was mentioned previously, the objective of most professional evaluation efforts is to develop better ways of delivering services to clients. However, there are instances when professional evaluation is undertaken to meet an administrative demand or to further one's own career. In these instances, once the evaluation data is organized, the practitioner will want to use his or her programming skills to try and ensure that this objective is achieved. The sharing of the evaluative data with agency administrators (if the data are positive) becomes a step in the program.

Practice Situations

Practice writing a plan to use the evaluation results. Develop the steps to the goal using a format similar to Table 19. Select as your goal one of the intermediary goals that you identified as related to one of your high-priority goals. Consider potential time lines and possible reinforcements you might use in the implementation of the program.

DEVELOPING AND IMPLEMENTING A PLAN TO USE THE RESULTS: A SUMMARY

Goal: To make sure that the goal for the evaluation process is achieved

1. Select the particular evaluation goal to be achieved (e.g., improve performance).

2. Make sure the goal is fully operationalized (including the needed level of performance).

3. Brainstorm and sequence the program steps necessary to achieve the goal.

4. Set time lines and reinforcements helpful in implementing the program.

RECYCLING THE EVALUATION PROCESS

The evaluation process is ongoing. The practitioner's improved performance on the goals points toward new goals, procedures, and results. Specifically, this book presents an approach to professional evaluation in which *many* client and administrative goals are identified and assigned priorities. For *some* of the highest priority goals, related intermediary goals are determined. These priority and intermediary goals are subsequently operationalized. The practitioner's performance is monitored, the results organized, and a plan to use the results developed. The practitioner's performance on the remaining goals that were initially identified still remain to be evaluated.

In implementing an evaluation process, the practitioner will necessarily choose to focus on a limited number of goals. After improving her or his performance on the initial goals, the practitioner can establish priorities for the remaining goals and recycle the evaluation process. By recycling the evaluation process, the practitioner may ultimately complete the evaluation of her or his performance on many of the goals that were originally set. Each time the practitioner has an opportunity to reexamine the original set of goals, she or he will again want to consider the rehabilitation process and administrative demands, needs, and wants. By the time the practitioner is ready to recycle the evaluation, the factors that went into the initial process of establishing priorities may have changed. Each time the evaluation process is recycled, the practitioner has an opportunity to view the larger picture of the total rehabilitation process.

Practice Situations

This is the time to review your understanding and expertise in systematic professional evaluation. Return to your list of client and administrative goals. Check to see if your priorities have changed. Complete the entire evaluation process for the next high-priority goal.

RECYCLING THE EVALUATION PROCESS: A SUMMARY

Goal: To enable the practitioner to repeat the professional evaluation process on other high-priority goals

1. If appropriate, establish a new list of client and administrative goals.

2. Establish new priorities for client and administrative goals.

3. Identify the related intermediary goals.

4. Operationalize the priority goals and related intermediary goals.

5. Develop and implement a monitoring plan.

6. Develop a scale to organize the results.

7. Develop and implement a plan to use the results.

8. Once again, recycle the evaluation process.

DEVELOPING NEW DIRECTION: A SKILLED APPROACH

From the window of her office at the rehabilitation agency, Diane could see harbingers of spring — a robin perched blissfully on the budding branch of a maple tree, leaves of green appearing on the parched grass, joggers prancing by. She could also feel, within herself, a sense of growth welling up. Today, she was to begin evaluating her performance on the final two goals of the nine she had originally set for herself.

The process had been hard work — setting goals, determining related intermediary goals, operationalizing the goals, developing and implementing a plan to monitor her performance, obtaining the results. Moreover, on four goals she had found her performance to be somewhat unacceptable. For these, she had identified her weaknesses and improved her performance on specific intermediary goals to the point where she had reached a necessary and satisfactory level of performance. This process of improving her performance was facilitated by the fact that she had thor-

oughly operationalized her goals earlier in the evaluation process.

Diane's agency had no systematic evaluation programs, and she felt the model she had used could be adapted by other practitioners to monitor and improve their rehabilitation performances. She decided to broach it at their weekly meeting this afternoon.

Looking at the paraphernalia on the desk — the list of goals, the monitoring plans, the scales to organize the results, the programs to improve her performance — Diane realized that, rather than finishing the process, she was actually beginning a new phase. Having mastered the skills of professional evaluation, she could now recycle the process, develop new client and administrative goals, and begin evaluating her performance on them. Evaluation could become, not sporadic and separate, but intrinsic to her job.

Returning her gaze to the robin, who sat immobile, basking in the warming sun, Diane felt that she had enhanced not only her rehabilitation performance, her delivery of services to clients, but also her potential for professional advancement. This, she felt, deserved some kind of reward. Seiji Ozawa was conducting the Boston Symphony at Tanglewood Saturday. Expensive? Yes. But she deserved it.

Before turning to her final goal, she saw the robin lift from the branch and float across the sky.

REFERENCES

Alden, J.   Evaluation in focus. *Training and Development Journal,* Oct. 1978, 45–50.

Anthony, W. A.   *Principles of psychiatric rehabilitation.* Amherst, MA: Human Resource Development Press, 1979.

Bucker, L.   Joint effect of feedback and goal setting on performance: A field study of residential energy conservation. *Journal of Applied Psychology,* 1978, *63,* 428–433.

Chu, F. D., and Trotter, S.   The madness establishement. In *Ralph Nader's study group report on the National Institute of Mental Health.* New York: Grossman, 1974.

Erez, M.   Feedback: A necessary condition for the goal-setting performance relationship. *Journal of Applied Psychology,* 1977, *62,* 624–627.

Flowers, J.   Goal clarity as a component of assertive behavior and a result of assertion training. *Journal of Clinical Psychology,* 1978, *34,* 744–747.

Hart, R.   Therapeutic effectiveness of setting and monitoring goals. *Journal of Consulting and Clinical Psychology,* 1978, *46*(6), 1242–1245.

Latham, G., and Rinne, S.   Improving job performance through training in goal setting. *Journal of Applied Psychology,* 1974, *59,* 187–191.

Smith, D. L.   Goal attainment scaling as an adjunct to counseling. *Journal of Counseling Psychology,* 1976, *23,* 22–27.

Spaniol, L.   A program evaluation model for rehabilitation agencies and facilities. *Journal of Rehabilitation Administration,* July 1977, *1*(2), 4–15.

Suchman, E.   *Evaluation research: Principles and practices in public service and social action programs.* New York: Russel Sage Foundation, 1967.

Walker, R. A.   The ninth panacea: Program evaluation. *Evaluation,* 1972, *1*(1), 45–53.

NOTES

NOTES